ROAD MAPS

Road Maps

Poetry and Prose

Margaret A. Westlie

Selkirk
STORIES

Printed by CreateSpace, an Amazon.com Company

.

Self

These little poems show the way.
With words and images I convey
   a sense of self.

A road map to the inner me,
   a path through pain and mystery,
   long road to health.

Directions for a valid life
   full lived as singleton and wife,
   signpost to wealth.

Wealth of spirit, wealth of heart,
   to live abundance is an art
   I owe myself.

Accidental Child

It was an accident, albeit a planned one.
But look what they created—
    a changeling child who never fits.
Doomed or blessed to travel with few companions of
    like mind.
The only transcendental child of accidental parents.

Baby Talk

My needs are few,
      my wants still fewer;
      a bite to eat,
      a place to lay my head.
I cry for you,
      but fad or fashion intervenes
      to let me weep alone.
Darkness hides discomfort,
      muffles my distress.
Abandoned to the cold and shadows
      of our northern night,
      I seek solace where it can't be found,
      and search my lifetime for what wasn't there.

Divine Intervention

I remember once having a long quarrel with my sister. It started after lunch and went on all afternoon both before and after a play we went to see at Queen Elizabeth High School—"Peter Pan," I think it was. We left the house in a natter with each other and yinged and yanged all the home. I have no idea anymore what the bone of contention was that day but the quarrel came to an abrupt end when we were changing back into our play clothes and I grabbed the hanger that she had taken down for herself. The hook caught in the bedspread and tore a very long strip right down the middle. My sister ran to tell and shortly thereafter my mother arrived with a piece of kindling stick about a foot long and an inch in diameter and proceeded to apply it to my backside. I could have used some divine intervention about then, although Hazel was giving a good representation of the avenging angel herself.

Making Me

Develop upper body strength they said.
It's the only way, in your condition, to lose weight.
Your metabolic rate is far too low
      to work without assistance.
Nine months I clamber up mountainous machines
      bought from the Dallas Cowboys.
I climb down on the other side when I am done.
I add aerobics to the mix this year.
Women make babies in nine months.
Making a new me is much more difficult.

Breakfast

I used to like my breakfast. I still do, although with less enthusiasm. It has come to represent the start of another day of denial. Not that I don't get enough to eat, but it's restricted to certain foods. Unfortunately, the food industry seems to be into torture with its myriad ads for fast foods and new desserts. Occasionally I see the devil's work in it. For instance, we were at the grocery store the other day and we had completed a perfectly agreeable shopping trip through the vegetable aisle and were going through the checkout. I had been following Dr. Phil's advice about not putting temptation in my own way. We took our turn through the checkout and the very last thing the cashier did was to wave an overflowing basket of a large assortment of freshly baked muffins in front of my eyes. "Would you like to try one of our muffins?" she asked as she sprouted horns.

My Own Song

Outside the seasons,
      earthbound for this,
      another year of mortal life,
      I see the ebb and flow of people
      bent on leading ordinary lives
      while I stand watching.
Helpless to break the barrier between us,
      I lead an extraordinary life
      that no one comprehends.

Not of this Earth

Sometimes I feel as if I am not of this earth. That I am only visiting here until it's time to go back to somewhere else. Back to where I came from.

Once I had my cards read and she said: "You came here from the stars." She was surprised. So was I. Until then I had only suspected it.

I have never belonged the way others have. It was always as if there was a veil between me and others. It's still there but I don't find it so hard to see through anymore. I drop into groups for a visit and then go back to my own place behind the curtain.

Aliens

We landed on Mars yesterday.
Scientific audacity got us there
    microbes and all.
Like tourists in some foreign capital,
    or Martians on reconnaissance to earth,
    we dig and snoop and take snapshots
    beside red rocks named Barnacle Bill and Yogi.
An American dream is realized;
    we have truly become the aliens.

Written in 1997

Hi Guys!

John and I are cloud watchers by day and star gazers by night, clouds permitting. We treated ourselves to the Perseid meteor shower this year and were suitably impressed. The black Wisconsin sky was sprinkled with stars, and we lay on our backs on the grass watching and waiting. The black flies waited with us.

Staring out into the darkness of the universe is a humbling experience. By day we are so taken up with our accomplishments that we never think about our tiny place in the greater Milky Way and beyond. At night the story is different.

My mind reviews all the science articles I can remember about space and gravity and other forces that keep our little blue planet in place. I sometimes have an awful vision of earth suddenly losing its power of gravity and bouncing away like a ping pong ball into outer space, narrowly missing our nearer neighbours as we pull on our sweaters and our winter coats. Should we wave at the aliens as we go past Mars?

John goes into the house to get another blanket while I wait uneasily on the lawn staring into the sky. I wish for selective vision so that I can screen out what I don't want to see by myself. The aliens wouldn't want a plump middle-aged writer like me, I reassure myself. If they did, they'd have come for me long ago. My uneasiness grows. John seems to be taking a long time. I wander toward the house and meet him coming back with Sport's dog blanket. John spreads the blanket and I return to my thoughts on the universe.

What about these little guys that other people say they see getting out of strange vehicles in the middle of the night? I feel safer to speculate on the problem now that I have company again. Are they real? It would seem they are, since enough sane people have seen them and reported them. People with impeccable credentials like United States presidents and senators have seen them. Aliens have been reported loitering above the White House and other important properties across the country. They've been picked up on radar for speeding too, although they haven't been ticketed yet.

My eyes are caught by the spectacular trail of a dying meteor. "They seem so close to us," I say to John. "I wonder if one would last until it reached us here in, Wisconsin?"

"Probably not," he replies, "they're not that big and they'd burn out before they got here. Besides, they're not coming from the right direction." He flings an arm around my shoulders and goes back to watching for meteors.

I scan the dark sky for the next one. They are about fifteen minutes apart. Not really a shower, more like a Scotch mist. I swat at a black fly. He's been trying to have supper for some time now. His wife joins him and I don't discriminate. I swat at her too.

I wonder if the aliens regard us in the same way that we regard black flies. If they do we're in big trouble. Maybe some do and others don't. I've learned that there are the Greys, and the Nordics and recently I've read about the brown furry ones with the long arms.

The Greys are the ones who are most often seen taking samples of flora and fauna. Flora wasn't too pleased about her ride in the space craft, but Fauna being fauna, didn't have much to say at all, since animals don't talk back.

The Nordics are the ones who look Norwegian. They're tall and blond and speak with an accent. They blend most easily with human beings, so even if they are here more often that the Greys, no one would notice.

The brown furry ones with the long arms look a lot like Alf and could easily hide out in a toy store, if they knew what a toy store was. Maybe they've investigated those too. Aliens are certainly busy enough in other areas, and getting busier every year, or so I hear. Ever since Kenneth Arnold first described their aircraft from his plane in 1947, they've been appearing all over the place.

Kenneth Arnold was a private pilot from Idaho who was flying near Mount Rainier in Washington state when he noticed nine silver discs cavorting at speeds of nearly one thousand miles per hour. For want of a better term he described them as upside-down teacup saucers and the name 'flying saucers' was born. This was a fortunate turn of events for the government that really didn't know what to do about its uninvited guests, and as we know now, couldn't have done much about them anyway. It gave the government the opportunity to pooh-pooh the whole idea of flying saucers and keep the phenomenon under wraps for years.

Unfortunately the phenomenon seemed to have a mind of its own, and an agenda which didn't coincide with that of the government. Maybe the aliens just didn't like being wrapped up, because no matter how much the authorities tried to destroy the credibility of the witnesses, more and more people saw these little people and their vehicles and believed. It almost seems as if the aliens want to be seen, and the more people who see them, the better it is for their purposes.

What do they want? I remember a science fiction program on television that showed a group of aliens making friends with a human. They offered to show him their planet and he agreed to go with them. When they arrived on the planet they escorted him to a perfect replica of his home on earth complete with a beautiful young woman. The aliens told him that they just wanted him to be comfortable while he was with them. They showed him around the house and offered him a drink of Scotch which he duly appreciated and then they left saying they would be back in time to take him to supper. To amuse himself in the meantime, he opened the living room drapes to get the view and discovered that the windows were barred and that a group of aliens stood outside staring back at him. He had become the latest acquisition in the local zoo!

Is that what we are to these people? A sort of zoo, or perhaps a giant experiment? They have certainly been seen taking plenty of samples and sometimes the whole animal, never mind the kidnapping of private citizens. From the reports of people who have merely been taken on a joy ride, such as it was, they have the upper hand when it comes to defence. Why haven't they used it on us before now?

Perhaps they don't want to. One of the more logical explanations that I've heard for their presence is that we are now at a point in our development where we can do tremendous damage not only to our own environment, but also to our immediate surroundings in space. We have only to think of the hole in the ozone layer for a very mild example of our cosmic carelessness. I expect that the dropping of the atom bomb did not go unnoticed in interplanetary circles either. I doubt that anyone has stopped to think what effect all the wars and rumours of wars may have had on the sleep of responsible aliens.

We now have the capacity to blow ourselves up and contaminate outer space, and, for all our education, we are a very aggressive and not a very spiritually or emotionally evolved people. If there is any doubt on this point, all a person needs to do for clarification is to turn on the afternoon talk shows. Even the host may be in danger of physical violence there. Prime time television is even worse, and all this is being broadcast to the heavens. An alien not understanding our culture could easily misinterpret what he sees. Even this human alien from just across the northern border felt it necessary to enquire into the crime rate of Waterville, Maine, before committing to employment there!

We are also just on the verge of having the technology to explore outer space. Perhaps the alien cultures which are so obviously monitoring us are trying to keep us from destroying any more of the greater space environment that we have already. Our tendency to shoot first and ask questions later may be an undesirable trait in the larger scheme of cosmic politics. It certainly is at home.

I swat at another black fly. It think it's a cousin this time. "This is a good night to see a UFO," I say to John. "Um," he replies, absorbed in watching for meteors. I persist in my own line of thought. "How d'you think we should greet them? D'you suppose there's a protocol, like greeting Queen Elizabeth, or would a pleasant wave and 'hi, guys' do?"

Grey Pages

My desk is clutter-free.
Not so my mind.
A cocklebur collecting trite it sprouts cliches,
    like Kennebec potatoes in the spring.

Like a ball of knitting yarn
    with knitting pins stuck in,
    an antennaed cartoon sputnik,
    launch-ready in my skull.

Thought people crowd the edges,
    each eager to be heard.
Not one real soul among them,
    tired dialogues in hand,
    they daily sprout cliches.
'Til trite becomes a river
    and smooths rough voices down
    to faded words and phrases
    that fill the page with grey.

Words

They dance in my brain,
    and sparkle and sing,
      they laugh and cry out to be heard.
They clamour for stardom
    like actors on stage,
      and play and cavort every day.
From neuron to neuron like acrobats
    they reach for their next trapeze.
When I'm wakeful at night the party's still on,
    my personal vaudeville revue.

Speed Reading

I savour words
    and try their divers textures on my tongue.
They slide past teeth and tonsils to my brain.
They integrate themselves into my awareness,
    and birth new feelings, cold and hot,
    or soothe and smooth like ice cream in July.
Speed reading dulls the edges,
    bypassing everything but facts.
It mists the surfaces like bottles on the ocean sand,
    obscuring bite and crisp and sparkle.
Words lose their perfect syllables to speed.

At Home with the Folks

My aunt's laughter is quiet in the summer dusk,
    gentle amusement at her own expense.
The subject changes. We share the news.
"Did you hear of Ian? He's diabetic, you know.
    But he's alright if he can still complain
    despite his age."
"It's sad about Mary and the cancer, though she knew."
The dusk grows somber.
"And Liz, too.
It took great courage to have both breasts removed."
"She's doing well, for all."
Shadows are alive with deep concern.
"She went back to work the next week. She's strong."
"Did you know our minister?"
I shake my head. "I've only heard of him."
"Well, he's dead.
Pneumonia took him,
    he wasn't old.
His life was full with family and friends
    and now he's dead.
It will be our turn next."

Sibling Rivalry

"Waste not want not," said big sister,
Stirring the last of the D-Con
Into baby brother's pablum.
"Yum, just like raisins.
Eat up like a good boy."
She scraped the plate clean.
"Remember the starving children in Biafra.
Momma said you're ours to keep.
Did you have enough breakfast?
Let's play hangman.
Momma says: 'Things done by halves
Are never done right.'
Here, let me tighten the noose."

My Father's Passing

He faded out of life.
I wasn't there,
    but then I wasn't there at his beginning.
He came to me one night,
    the trip—two thousand miles.
An instant journey of the other self.
He seemed pleased to see me, and with himself.
Of his three children
    I'm the one who sees continuance of life,
    not here, but on the other side.
We'll have a great reunion when we meet again.

Confluence

I have been reading a lot about reincarnation lately. It's a fascinating subject; one that rings quite true for me. It reminds me of rivers flowing into larger rivers and brooks flowing into larger brooks. The flow of life joins other lives and melds with hardly a ripple. Sometimes it creates rapids and separates into two channels, to rush pellmell into another life again.

At the confluence of rivers is great beauty. On the quieter meetings, trees hang over the banks giving shade to the fish that ride the small currents along the shore. Sometimes where larger rivers meet, the beauty is rugged and the water rough and filled with snags. It takes wisdom and experience to navigate the rapids and arrive safely at port once again.

Reincarnation is like that, in that we flow and drop into the snags and rapids of a life, and with wisdom and common sense emerge into spirit once again.

Grieving

This pain I feel,
      is it the burgeoning of grief?
Grief for a past I never loved,
      for friendships lost or dying
         on the vine of distance,
      for situations unrepaired and unrepairable,
      misunderstood and tossed
         upon the midden heap of time.
Tears compost days, like leaves, into new growth.
A fecund labouring mind turns pain to riches,
      far greater than the want of former years.

North Atlantic Homecoming

Chill November rain slants in from grey Atlantic.
Fog horns defy slow creeping mist to no avail.
Container ships ghost past the harbour mouth
      to seek safe haven in oily dark of winter berth.
Fog-muffled glow of street lights leads me home
      up streets with optimistic names.
Spring Garden, Jubilee and Summer Streets
      anticipate the warmth of future seasons.
North on prosaic Robie Street,
      home lights inspire my step.
Through steam damp windows kitchen light
      illuminates my mother's supper work.
Salt cod and pork scraps, potatoes in blue jackets,
      sweet turnip mashed to golden pap.
A North Atlantic winter feast
      dispels damp evening gloom.

Fog

It seeps in, cold as death,
      blurring the edges of reality.
Street lamps share their auras
      with lone passersby,
        bestowing unearned halos round their heads.
Nearby, in the mist, cars skid and touch,
      not gently, on rain slick streets.
A siren sounds from somewhere close at hand,
      mixing with sombre hoots of freighters
      ghosting past the lighthouse into open sea.

Cardigan Bay

The farther shore half-hides within the heat haze of July.
A cats-paw breeze caresses from the south
      and lifts up summer clouds in summer skies.
Slow-moving in its chosen, airy place,
      the seagull holds a steady course
      and calls his lonely cry across the bay.
A locust whines from nearby spruce,
      and noisome seaweed crackles on the strand
      as whitecaps haste across the sun-soaked bay
      to die in sussuration on the shore.
This refuge from the noise of life is mine.
A safe retreat kept close in memory.
I wander barefoot over sun-warmed sands
      and sate soul hunger for ancestral home.

Written in 1995

Night Driving on the Island

Our headlights sweep red ditches free of night.
Behind us, darkness billows in to hide our way.
From Little Sands to Charlottetown
    cocooned in Island peace, we ride secure
    past farms already dark with sleep.
Dogs herald our swift passage with three barks
    and then go back to chasing rabbits in the dark.
Beige foxes watch from bushes, then turn tail
    and slink into the undergrowth
    as if guilty of some nighttime crime.
Above, cold stars withhold their little lights,
    and we roll on toward midnight and safe home.

Prince Edward Island Sunshine

The sunshine here is like no other sunshine.
It has a quality of gold
      that burnishes the trees
      and brick red soil,
      and modifies the scene in every season.
Red and green in summer,
      red and white in winter,
      with fields sewn round with fences,
      and ox-eye daisies in the fall.

County Line Road

Damp red road, cool on bare feet,
    through trees that touch their branches overhead.
Mud in puddle bottoms squishes through city toes,
    water cools our feet and stains them red.
The scent of fern is on the air,
    sweet and spicy, almost like dessert.
Birds chirp and flutter in the trees,
    then grow briefly silent as we pass.
Is this the way to heaven?
We don't know.
For now it seems the only way to go.

Mist on the River

Mist lies heavy on the river.
The farther shore is hidden from my view.
Twelve feet of snow is slowly melting;
  as deep as that and more will have to go
  before we see the ground again in springtime.
The season long awaited will be slow.
The birds outside are always ever hopeful.
Blue jays wet with springtime rain fly low.
Trees in bud are eager for the sunshine.
Tomorrow is supposed to bring more snow.
My garden's buried deep beneath a snowdrift;
A late lie-in for plants, but then who knows?
Perhaps they're ready waiting under snowbanks.
They may not see real sunshine until June.

Lingering Light

Light lingers longer on a winter evening,
     hinting that the spring is nearly here.
Despite the constant cold of winter
     dreams of gentler warmer days appear.

Snow and ice still frozen on the sidewalk,
     Christmas just departed from our minds,
Plans for summer gardens slowly surface,
     we mark seed catalogues with our finds.

January thaw will be upon us,
     then only a short sprint to early spring.
One more northeast gale will snow us under
     then crocus, geese and robins will be king.

Moonshine

The moon shines full at midnight.
Nothing stirs.
Shadows lie in stark relief against the lawn.
Blades of grass stand stiffly
        like new spiked hair.
It's almost bright as day.

But blue is the colour of the night:
        a soft grey blue like ancient drugstore rinses.
Old ladies know the colour.
It hides the yellow tones of age
        and covers well the deeds of day and night.

Walking Home at Night

Hunched into our parkas we walk the red road together, our heads still bare because it is not yet winter. Overhead the milky way washes a wide swathe of stars across the heavens as if an artist had dipped his brush into sparkles and splashed them across the sky. Somewhere nearby in the woods an owl hoots. It is a comforting sound in the darkness. Under our feet fallen leaves crunch and crackle as we crush them in our passing. A rustle in the dry grasses of the ditch gives away the hiding place of a mouse or a vole. With soft clatter of wings the owl soars and drifts on the thermals looking for his supper. Suddenly he dives into the grass, talons ready. There is a tiny squeak and the owl rises out of the darkness, a small forest creature silhouetted in his beak. To the east the moon rises, silent and orange over our way home.

River Fishing

Moored against the current
    he casts his line
    then sits motionless
    silhouetted by the rising sun.
This daily ritual lasts 'til sunset
    when mosquitoes drive him in
    despite repellent.
A search for peace seems to be his aim.
But peace from what?
Creditors?
A carping wife?
His own dread thoughts?
Fishing's a pretext.
Summer and winter his line lies slack.
But at least the fish are safe.

Night Shift

I pass the mirror and glance aside
    to see the person reflected there.
The figure is stocky,
    I know it's me,
    "une femme forte" as they say in Paris.
A sturdy girl and strong,
    able to work long hours once,
    but that was long ago.
Working nights has taken its toll;
    disrupted the inner clock.
All these years hence
    still wakeful at night
    and drowsy during the day.

No Secrets, Please

I don't like secrets.
They weigh me down
      and fill my gut with bowling balls.
I rarely trust to share my own,
      and even less a friend's.
Once a secret's shared it's not a secret.
We're connected to the world
      by seven degrees.

Decisions

Shall I go here?
Or better there?
Maybe neither one.
Where will each one lead?
Will I do well or ill?
Decisions are so hard to make,
      we cannot see the end.
Decide by not deciding
      leaves too much up to fate,
      like riding in a car that's lost its brakes.

Hesitation

He who hesitates is lost. Look before you leap. These are two contrary ideas that negate each other. I am of the opinion that it's better to leap first and look later, unless it's off a tall building or a high cliff. Hesitation destroys the excitement of discovery. Throw caution to the winds, as they say, and experience those winds as cleansing and enlivening. Soar to new heights on them. Discover new ideas, new gifts. Reach your fullest potential, like a sail billowing full of wind. Be alert to new experiences. Don't ignore the little things. Sometimes they lead to the best events of one's life.

Politics

They cross-accuse
        and self-defend.
One says this,
        the other that.
And on it goes,
        a tit for tat.

A tat for tit,
        a mortal blow.
A who said what,
        the other no.

Which one's the best?
We'll never know,
        but surely one will strike the blow
        to win his case,
        to send the other to defeat
        and take his seat.

Mystic Melody

Today I heard a mystic melody.
Notes from an under-tuned piano
      rang in my mind's ear.
It should not have been;
      no one was there.
I wrote them down
      to keep them from escaping,
      back to the ether from whence they came.

No

No!
A barren word, empty of promise.
Cold as Greenland at the winter solstice.
Soul-chilling, heart-shattering, mind-numbing.
No rising to warm life.
No room for "what if" or "let's."
No plan,
    no bloom,
    unless you count dead asters in the fall.

Always and Never

Always and never are absolutes. They are also elusive. Since Einstein fiddled with our concept of time and space, always and never have lost their meaning. Take always as an example. How can you say I always do such and such when time isn't linear or if it doesn't exist? This will hold true of never too. If all that exists is now, always and never are non-existent except in our minds. They are concepts of convenience. Past and future are whatever we're not doing now. It's like a follow spotlight. The only reality is what is currently being lighted.

Hold Still the Silence

Hold still the silence.
The clamour of loud minds and verbal droolings
        clutters the air; invades our precious space.
Those who lead where it's better not to go
        are best ignored.
Clear minds make clear decisions.
Guard well against polluted pratings
        and rotten rhetoric.
Remember who you are.

Burdens

The load is heavy.
Too heavy now to bear.
For fifteen years I've carried them,
  your secrets and your fears.
Your choices are not fruitful.
I've nothing left to share.
I have no strength,
  I can't go on.
My health is frail because
  I've carried you too long.
So travel on without me;
  good luck and peace be yours.
I give you to the universe,
  for your remaining years.

Stopping Short

Most things can be stopped, short of death and TNT. Even runaway trains can be stopped although not pleasantly. The whole idea has an ominous ring. Where does one go with it? If one dwells on it long enough it could lead to the mental ward, and then what? Convincing the world of one's sanity after a sojourn on Unit 9 is not easy. People tend to treat people who have had "mental issues" with delicacy as if shielding them from stress will forestall their distress and another visit to the farm. Emily Dickinson got it right when she wrote:

> Much madness is divinest sense
> To a discerning eye;
> Much sense the starkest madness.
> T"is the majority
> In this, as all, prevails.
> Assent, and you are sane;
> Demur, — you're straightway dangerous,
> And handled with a chain.

Poetry by Emily Dickinson courtesy www.public-domain-poetry.com.

Collusion

I did not know you when you called.
I do not know you now.
Your story told too much too soon.
I feel that I've colluded in your sin.

You love your sin.
It's all you think about.
You need to let it rest.
It will be no less sinful in a year or two;
        just easier to manage.

Absolution's what you want.
You can't say sorry yet.
You have to pick the scab and make it bleed.
And bleed it will
        until the sin's resolved
        and fades to scars.

Recognition

It should have been permanent.
The separation, I mean.
But he came bearing lobsters and a sad face.
So we cooked the lobsters and I gave in.
Four long years of catastrophe;
        I should have known.
Then more long years looking for home,
        until there's nowhere to go but away.
Away to make wondrous discoveries.
Talented wise-woman,
        overflowing with joy,
        I do not recognize him any more.

Small Mistakes

They stick together and become prickly, sticky balls like twine collections or burdocks. Then they take on a life of their own and gain momentum as if rolling downhill. Sisyphus would know what I am talking about—he had lots of practice pushing his rock uphill only to see it roll, crashing and bouncing, to the bottom again, flattening everything in its path. He could only shrug and do it all over again, and again, and again.

That's the problem with small mistakes—they multiply. Rabbits have nothing on them. One small mistake can ruin a whole day or a whole lifetime. Take marriage for example. One tiny "yes," said when we are not thinking straight, can lead to a lifetime of trying to make it right when it wasn't right to begin with. Sisyphus knows.

Leavings

This was left when he was gone:
    a box of special stationery
    valued by him for its thickness and bite.
He fancied himself a gentleman
    with deer-stalker cap and caped overcoat.
He smoked a pipe too,
Though only when he was writing his damned letters
    to everyone but me.

The Last Night

On the last night I saw an old friend—at least I thought he was a friend—we had coffee together and he insulted my portraits by calling them "your little sketches." I set him straight several times then realized where my former lack of confidence arose from. Since then, I have learned not to apologize for what I do creatively. It is what it is, and I am what I am, and anyone who can't see the worth of it all can take a long walk off a short pier. So there!

Change Ringing

Church bells from the village
    are joyfully ringing the change.
Across the river and up the drive
    I listen and watch the sun glow fade
    from day bright gold to green.
It gently settles on the mist
    as purple as fairy tales.
The farms emerge as if afloat
    among the hills and trees;
    the cattle low as they wander home
    clanging their bells in counterpoint
    to church bells across the fields.

England 1992

Ancient Graves

The wind blows idly 'cross the ancient graves.
It touches first the oldest of them all,
    then wanders out and blesses every one
    amid the daisies and the buttercups.

Long centuries have passed since last they strolled
    mourning those who'd gone before their time.
And now we walk and wonder at their loss,
    and wonder more at what they'd left behind.

Is their life's work of value to us now?
Will ours be worth a future passing glance?
Or does it even out at death's appointment,
    and matter to us only while we're here?

England 1992

Cemeteries

They are reflective places. I read gravestones and wonder how anyone could call their child Missouri Sally Ann; or what happened to the seven children in one family who died at young ages but years apart? Some forward looking people have their stones already engraved with their names and dates of birth, awaiting only their day of death that has not happened yet.

Cemeteries hide the first kiss in the darkness of a late fall evening. The wind soughs through the fir trees, the smell of autumn is in the air and its sound is underfoot. The moon is hardly visible between the branches of the oaks that are home to squirrels and birds during the shortening days. The soft touch of lips barely beyond childhood, damp and tentative in the firstness of it; cheeks pressed close and cold with impending winter; cold as the stone they sit on while they forget who lies below. She once had a first kiss too and now can kiss no more. Ashes to ashes, dust to dust, if the Lord doesn't get you then the devil must. I wonder where she went?

Pheasant Hunting

There's something carnal in men's minds,
    a need for blood.
Old men with greying, thinning hair
    take aim at harmless birds.
And laugh, exultant, when one falls,
    like boys at play.

The shooter does not have to hunt,
    he merely aims.
The beater does the work of raising birds.
Their hiding place revealed, the rest is easy.
One bullet leaves them lying where they fall,
    no use as food.

Such wanton waste of God's good work
    without a cause.
We have no need of game at any time.
The butcher shop supplies our needs in every season.
What sport is there in taking aim
    at hapless birds?

England 2008

Bish and Shelly

Duck pond's empty now,
  green with water weeds.
Waterfall and ducks no longer there.
Quaint cottage gone,
  and in its place two mansions.
Half a million pounds apiece or so they say.
Money talks;
  to some mere babbling.
At least the ducks had names.

England 2008

November Wind

Wind rumbles in the chimneys
    and riots in the eaves.
It rushes round the corners
    and rattles window panes.

Before the gale, trees loose their leaves
    to scud and dip and dive.
Like children new released from school
    they hide and seek and leapfrog across lawns.
They scurry under hedgerows,
    small animals at bay.

I like to stand and watch the wind
    sweep clean and dust the woods.
Nature's keeping house
    the way I wish I could.

England 2008

English Breakfast

Delights of sausage
    still sizzling from the pan.
Black pudding, bacon
    and fried tomato slice.
A choice of bread,
    both brown and white,
    accompanied by jam.
A pain au chocolat, a raisin roll,
    croissants like crescent moons
    all butter-flaked and warm.
Life, rich in choices,
    waits but for my call.

American Breakfast

Bacon limp in liquid lard,
    home fries with cheese,
    pale scrambled eggs,
    biscuits with gravy
    cold as the greying lumps
    of last spring's snow.
And greyer still, but hot
    and just as lumpy,
    oatmeal porridge.
Look there! Bright fruit
    in slices on display.
Oh, dear, that child has sneezed
    and wiped his nose
    with hands that reach for cantaloupe.

Missouri Nights

Cool breeze blows across hot skin.
Cicadas play their fiddles in the trees.
The brook purls over rocks
    shining with moonlight borrowed
      through the oaks.
Cattle low, calling to newborn calves
    to keep them safe from coyotes on the prowl.
An owl hoots from a branch then soars away
    to ride the thermals round and round,
      then dives.
A squeak, and dinner is assured,
    at least for now.

Opera of Coyotes

I hear a train in the distance.
It could be north or south.
It haunts the level crossings,
    and sets the coyotes singing on the hill.
The dogs next door whose rusty barks
    cannot compare with coyotes singing parts,
        join in the chorus.
The opera continues,
    long after trains pass by,
    until actors tire and leave us
        waiting for just one more.

Autumn

Luminescent leaves glow golden
    in the slant of autumn sun.
Grackles clatter in high branches,
    then lift and soar as one ethereal body.
They leave behind silence,
    waiting for the dark and cold of winter.
Soon to come, it will snow
    upon the memories of summer
    when cicadas sawed and whined in midnight heat.
Now only owls and coyotes
    break the silence of the darkening year.

Not Deep Enough

Soon grass will grow over your new-made grave.
It will not be enough to hide the scars
    and heal the wounds that you inflicted.
The evil that you did lives on
    in hearts too young, too old to understand.
No grave is deep enough to hide your sin,
    Satan won't have you.
He's too good to touch your filthy soul.
Even oblivion is closed to you.
So there you lie, only six feet deep
    like everyone else.

Original Sin

One sinful act is all it took
    to ban me from the garden.
It wasn't me,
    why should I pay
    for Adam's disobedience?

Four thousand years,
    we still feel guilt,
    though it's not ours to shame us.
I don't see why,
    I wasn't there.
My conscience's clear on that one.

I have my sins that I commit.
I don't need help from Adam.
They are my choice,
    they are not God's.
It's up to me to clear them.

God said as much in olden times.
He cast our sins to salty depths.
We are sin free,
    we're not defiled.
John said so in plain language.

Passing Acquaintance

With a wink, a smile and a nod you left.
We watched you go.
We heard you greet Aunt Joan and Poppa,
    Uncle Dan and Momma,
      and others whose names we didn't catch.
You looked back once.
"They're all here," you said,
    and turned away once more.
Holding out your arms for hugs
    we heard you laugh and say: "Let's party!"

Out of the Corner of my Eye

I caught a flash of orange
       from the corner of my eye.
An ageing face above it smiled.
Ascended master of an ancient way
       of looking, thinking, saying.
Am I a heretic because I like to search for God?
Not everyone agrees,
       but that's okay with me.
We'll see who's right in eternity.

Behind Closed Doors

The door is closed.
I listen carefully for words I cannot hear,
    the truth of which I cannot understand.
The Gnostics had it,
    at least they thought they did.
God is present everywhere.
Yahweh storms and rants, judges and condemns.
He's not God.
He only thinks he is.
It's hard to tell standing on the wrong side of the door.

Divine Flow

Moving freely,
> moving gently
> on the flow of the Divine.

Leaving, leaving,
> friends and family,
> the old memories resign.

Learning, learning,
> ever searching
> for the answers from within.

Growing, growing
> like a flower
> reaching life beyond my ken.

Freedom of War

What price we pay to gain another's freedom.
We teach them peace with war.
Their country desolate, destroyed,
    their families scattered.
And still they look to us for respite and relief.

We say we're fair,
    but what is fair about destruction?
Old monuments are ground to powder with a bomb.
We cannot count the lives forever crushed in conflict,
    and death is not the worst that we can bear.

We are crusaders there like any army,
    intruding in a land that's not our own.
One bullet should suffice to bring them freedom,
    to take the evil tyrant from his throne.
One sniper could have done it with one bullet,
    and left the country clear to rise once more.

He and She

She does not raise her eyes to him across the booth,
    nor he raise his to hers.
Grim brows hold taut against expression.
Mouths inverted from long years of sufferance
        and undigested anger
      crunch carrot sticks and celery.
Hands busy with knife and fork avoid the space
    between the plates of crudités.
They eat and tamp their mutual loathing down
      with sticks of bread,
    and hone their dentures on the silence.

In a Café

We borrow so many words from the French and then declare them our own. Take *café*, for instance. One might say in English that one was in a coffee but that makes no sense. The coffee is in us. Which reminds me of Blake and his tiger. Or maybe it wasn't Blake, because the rhyme I'm thinking of is a limerick about a lady riding out on the back of a tiger but coming home on the inside. I wonder if a liger or a tion would be confused about it, given that they are cross-bred with each other. I wonder if they are ever transgendered? What a mix-up that would be!

Buried Treasure

My contact with the elderly outside of institutions had been limited to a few demanding and decrepit ex-in laws, and my grandmother who, at one hundred plus years of age, was neither decrepit nor demanding. That January day I was not looking for a geriatric friend and had no intention of encouraging one. Leta changed all that.

I could see when she introduced herself to me eight years ago that she was determined to make friends, and, much to my dismay, I was not going to be able to avoid it. My heart fell even further when she told me that she had a husband, who is both sick and blind, living at home, and that in fact, the poor man was dying, and would I like to come up and visit sometime soon? I did not hurry.

I would greet her when I would see her in her yard, thinking that was really as close to any neighbour as I wanted to be, especially one of that vintage. She invited me in one day to show me something or other. I stayed for a brief visit and over the course of the next eight years I discovered the buried treasure that is Leta.

Leta is at present seventy-seven. She was the fourth child in a family of six. She was a wife to Ralph for fifty-three years, and a mother to three children, two of whom have lived to reach adulthood. She has five grandchildren and two great-grandchildren. These are the bare bones of her life. Leta is more than this.

Her greatest dream was to finish high school, have a career and make something of herself, and although she had several chances, marriage was not high on her list of important things to do with her life. In her last year of formal schooling when she was just fifteen, she went with a younger brother to the basketball game. There were no buses to ride in, so the man who trucked cattle lined his cattle truck with benches and took everyone to the game in the back of the truck. His assistant was Ralph, her future husband. At their destination, when she climbed down from the truck, she tripped over a rope. Ralph helped her to her feet.

"I always said that I fell for him." She smiles at the memory. "I didn't know who helped me that night, and I didn't see him again for four years. I didn't even know it was him until long after we were married!"

Leta has a high regard for learning. Her dream to finish high school and have a career was spoiled by the Depression. Her father was a farmer and money was scarce. She finished grade nine and went to work, and met Ralph again. They married and had their family, but she still wanted a career.

"Ralph said I could get a job if I could find one where I could be here to see the children off to school in the morning and be here when they came home at night. He really didn't want me to take one. He thought that I wouldn't be able to find one with those hours. He thought he was safe." She chuckled at the idea. "But I was determined! I looked and looked and finally I saw an ad for a part time worker in the old high school cafeteria. I worked from ten to one every day for the first year, then they offered me the position of supervisor. I worked there for twenty-eight years."

She now had her career, but she still wanted to finish high school. In 1960, when her daughter was seventeen, Leta began studying to finish her education. She did it by correspondence course. When a question on her homework baffled her one evening she asked her daughter to help her. Her daughter said, "Mom, you'll never learn anything if I tell you the answers." Leta did her own homework and she earned her high school diploma.

Leta is a wonderful person to tell a joke to. She takes everything very seriously, especially jokes, if you don't prepare her for them. I told her a David Koresh joke that was floating around at the time of the incident in Waco, Texas.

"Leta, d'you know what David Koresh was wearing when they found him after the fire?"

Leta leaned over the arm of her chair with a quizzical expression on her face. "No, what was he wearing?"

"A smoking jacket and matching charcoal trousers."

"Was he now?" And then she got it and laughed and laughed, as much at herself as at the joke.

We were having a discussion about contraception the other evening and I made the comment that a person could always use aspirin.

"Oh," she said, "I didn't know you could do that. Aspirin, you say!"

"Yes," I replied, "you hold it tightly between your knees."

It was a delight to watch her face and hear her laugh as she realized the joke.

That's one of the nice things about Leta. I can talk to her about everything. Her years in Sunday School and her good common sense show her what the world is really all about and her advice is invaluable. She carries that good sense with her everywhere.

My husband and I invited her to visit us during a stay in England. She was only seventy-five then. We told her that she would have to be able to walk at least five miles a day at a brisk pace or it would not be worth her while to come. She was determined. She rode her exercise bicycle and walked in the mall every day all winter until she came to us in March. When she arrived she could walk faster than we could. I almost lost her in the London Underground. I took her to Nottingham to see Robin Hood and almost lost her there too. She climbed The Steep Hill in Lincoln, a perpendicular street leading to the cathedral, without stopping for breath. I have pictures of her on the way up.

She wanted me to take all of her pictures. She had had cataract surgery and did not see very well. We would point out details on buildings and monuments that we thought she should see. Her response was always: "Oh, isn't that pretty!" in the same tone of voice for everything. I was convinced that she would never keep everything straight and know which was which by the time she got home. When she showed the pictures to me on our return, every one was neatly labelled with an explanatory note on the back and they were all correct. I should not have doubted her.

Over the eight years of our friendship, for I can call it that now, I have discovered that Leta is artistic with an excellent eye for colour. Her quilts could win prizes. She has a wonderful fund of stories that she willingly shares on request. She loves to fish and frequently goes fishing with her aunt at Lake of the Ozarks. The broken ribs she sustained when she fell off the dock neither spoiled her enthusiasm, nor slowed her down. She volunteers at the hospital, a job into which she had to be persuaded, even though she really wanted to do it. She has a slight speech impediment and, "they won't be able to understand me." She did just fine and truly enjoys it as I knew she would. It is in her nature to help others.

The elderly people to whom I have devoted a large part of my working life were interesting people. I shared their end-of-life experiences with them and listened to their stories. However, the institutions in which I found them offered them up to me as if they were museum pieces to be carefully studied and returned to the shelf at the end of the day. Leta changed all that, and I am richer for it.

Written in 1993

Leta

How shocking!
Two accidents in one day.
Leta, who daily rides her bike
      and drives with care,
      is shattered.
Her confidence rushed away
      like water from the broken radiator.
Confusion dims her ancient eyes.
She looked mortality in the face
      and saw her death reflected there.

Flight of Life

I look into your eyes once bright with wit.
Today, dull with confusion, they look inward.
You go where I can't follow,
    though I would try if I could bring you back.
I strive to keep your attention, but it wanders,
    and so do you.
Lost in familiar places,
    I try to keep you with me, but I fail.
I'll always fail.
You're being paged,
    and you must go alone.

The Other Side

Where have you gone, grandma dear? We miss you on this side of the veil. Is the other side as it is described in the Bible? Are there really pearly gates? Did St. Peter greet you and open the gates for you? Did you learn to play the harp? Have you seen my friend Leta? She's a good person to know. She's got a lot of fun in her. We always liked her and enjoyed spending time with her. She told the minister who did her eulogy that she had felt herself to be out of her body and looking down on herself in her bed. He told us about it and I was most surprised as he is a Baptist minister and they are not known for their imagination or receptivity to things ethereal. Was it a sign for me to let me know that I am on the right track?

Learn more about Margaret Westlie,
her life and her books, at
www.margaretwestlie.com,
or scan the following QR code:

www.ingramcontent.com/pod-product-compliance
Lightning Source LLC
LaVergne TN
LVHW051814080426
835513LV00017B/1951